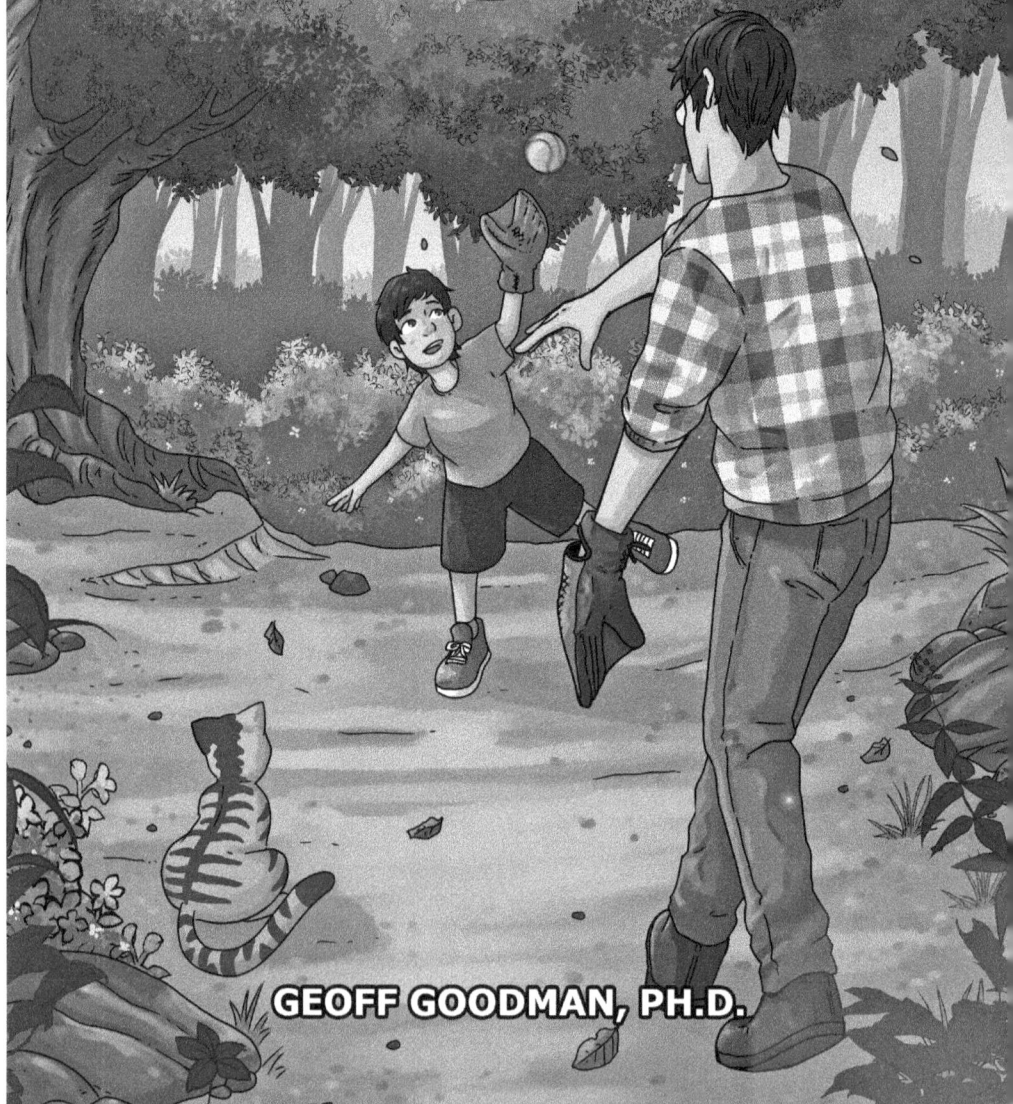

Junk in the Trunk
published by Walker Inspirations

PO Box 1055
North Lakes, 4509
Queensland Australia
www.trunkbook.info

First published as Daddy's Secret Cedar Chest in 2013
Republished as Junk in the Trunk in 2022

Written by Dr. Geoff Goodman, 2022
Editing by Liz Walker & Ali Stegert
Design by Jane Maughan, Creative Peek

This publication is designed to provide helpful information to our readers relating to prevention of pornography harms. This book is not intended as a substitute for the advice or services of mental health or other professionals. Content is provided in good faith to improve online child protection measures, raise awareness, and be used as a family & counselling tool. Readers and their carers are responsible for their own choices, actions, and results.

The publisher and the individual author disclaim responsibility for any adverse consequences which may occur directly or indirectly as a result of using or applying any contents within this publication.

Printed and distributed through Ingram Spark
Publishing Cataloguing-in-Publication Data

Creators:	Geoff Goodman, author
Title:	Junk in the Trunk
ISBN:	978-0-9580279-9-1
Target Audience:	Children aged 6-10-years-old
Subjects:	Online Safety
	Protective Behaviours
	Autonomy in children
	Juvenile literature

My buddy Billy always wins at hide-and-seek, but this time we were playing at my house. While I sneaked away to hide, Billy counted in the living room. "One... Two..." Knowing him, he'd already peeked to see which way I went.

As slinky as a cat, I scurried up the stairs, skipping over the creaky steps to the best hiding spot ever.

"11... 12..." Billy's voice carried up the stairs.

Just to throw him off, I rattled the knob on my bedroom door without going in. He'd search high and low through my bedroom. Meanwhile, I'd be curled up in my super-sneaky hidey-hole. I tiptoed further down the hall, stopping in front of Dad's room. Carefully, I turned the knob and slipped inside.

Under the window sat an old trunk, the trickiest hiding spot I'd ever dreamed up. Dad's bashed-up army trunk was perfectly kid-sized.

"18, 19, 20. Ready or not, here I come!" Downstairs, doors banged as Billy started his hunt. A moment later, he thundered up the stairs.

Yikes! No time to lose. I threw open the lid. Oh no! Messy junk filled the trunk to the brim. I took a magazine off the top of the pile.

Whoa, weird! The woman on the cover had no clothes on.

I opened the well-worn pages to the middle of the magazine. That lady was even more naked.

Wedged between piles of old magazines were DVDs with strange titles. Wait, what? We don't even watch DVDs anymore. What is all this stuff? Why did Dad have so many pictures and movies of naked bodies?

I looked a bit closer, and jammed in between the DVDs was an iPad. My heart pounded so loud I thought it might explode. Swiping the screen, it opened on one big tangle of arms and legs. I couldn't stop staring—what are these people doing? It didn't make sense. Whatever it was, my head buzzed, and my tummy felt weird—as if I'd just climbed off a roller coaster. Ughhh! This was crazy.

The door flung open. I jumped, threw the iPad down, and slammed the trunk shut.

"Ha! Found ya!" Billy yelled. "Cheater. You said this room was off limits." He tagged me. "You're it." He darted down the hall. His thumping feet almost drowned out the pounding of my heart.

I sat on the trunk to calm myself.

Billy ran back. "Come on, Jaden. You're it." He tilted his head and pointed at the trunk. "What's in there?"

My cheeks burned. "Nothing. Just... junk." I slid off the trunk, wishing the carpet would swallow me up. "I don't want to play inside anymore."

He shrugged and took off, hollering over his shoulder, "Last one to the trampoline is a rotten egg!" He scampered down the stairs, yelling something about getting snacks. I closed the door to Dad's bedroom. I wish I'd NEVER opened that trunk of junk.

Dinner was spaghetti and meatballs. I pushed the food around on my plate. No matter where I looked, I kept seeing the weird things I saw on the iPad. My legs wriggled and twitched. Why did I feel so strange?

Mom narrowed her eyes at me. "Did you and Billy fill up on snacks this afternoon?"

I shook my head. "Where's Dad?" As usual, his chair was empty, and the food in front of it was growing cold.

Mom rolled her eyes and speared a meatball on her plate. "Where do you think?"

His study. He spent so much time in there, and the door was always locked. I slouched down in my chair. Billy's dad ate dinner with his family every night and played catch with Billy and his little sister all the time.

Dad and I used to play board games together. Not anymore. It had been ages since he'd read me a story before bed. And he promised to help me learn to do flips on the trampoline.

Oh no! My eyes burned. I blinked and wiped at them so Mom wouldn't see the tears and get all worried. I swallowed, but my throat didn't work right. It was like swallowing gravel.

Mom saw everything. She sighed and took my plate without even lecturing me for not finishing my dinner.

She slid a dessert plate in front of me. On it was warm apple pie with ice cream melting around it. "Here. This should help. It's your favorite," Mom said, rubbing my hair.

I pushed it away. My tummy hurt.

Mom sat down close to me. "Okay, spill. What's wrong, Jaden?"

Before I could stop myself, the secret poured out of my mouth. "I found a stash of weird magazines in the trunk in Dad's bedroom. And then, I saw what was on the iPad."

Mom took a deep breath. "Oh Jaden..."

Oh no. Was she mad at me? Upset? She blinked her eyes a lot.

"I am so sorry that you saw what was in that trunk, and I'm furious at Dad for having it."

"I feel sick to my stomach," I whispered.

Mom patted my arm and frowned. "Yeah, so do I," she shot back. "Did Billy see everything?"

I shook my head.

"That's good, at least..." She looked at me, sternly. "Jaden, you know we have a rule about our bedroom being off limits." Sighing again, Mom went on. "I know this has made you feel bad and it might be confusing, but one thing is for sure—this is NOT your fault. Okay?"

I nodded.

"You go get a bath, and I'll deal with your father." She gave me a hug but not the warm and fuzzy kind. I could tell she was just about to blow.

I took my plate to the sink and went upstairs. When I reached the top step, I heard Mom knocking on the study door.

"Derrick, open the door. We have to talk. Now!" Her voice was shrill. She started pounding on the door.

I froze. I'd never heard Mom talk so angrily.

"I can't take this anymore! Why do you have to look at that garbage? First it was magazines and DVDs, but I can't believe you carelessly left an iPad for your son to find! What's that going to do to him? I'm left to pick up the pieces while whatever habit you're into online is costing us a fortune. Have you seen our credit card bills? How are we going to pay them off?"

Dad swore and yelled something back. My cat Nahla darted up the stairs, straight past me into my room. Under my bed was her favorite hiding place when she was afraid.

Mom cried, "I'm going to throw your laptop out the window. And you're next!"

Even with covered ears, I could still hear them yelling. I rushed to my bedroom on wobbly legs. Eventually, Nahla crept out from under the bed to be with me. Snuggled under the covers on my bed, I stroked her soft fur. She purred and rubbed her head against my hand.

What bad thing had I done? All I did was open Dad's old army trunk. I shouldn't have told Mom what I saw.

Downstairs, doors slammed. Voices yelled on and on. My eyelids felt heavier and heavier...

The lid on the old trunk rose slightly. A hairy hand slid out of the crack; its finger beckoned. Dad stood watching. He lifted the lid and stared at the creature inside.

I saw it too—a terrible tangled monster with two heads, lots of hair, and so many arms and legs, all snaked together, growing and tangling. I couldn't understand it, no matter where I looked. My heart raced, and it was hard to breathe—I just wanted to escape before something happened.

Dad kept staring, but he wasn't scared at all. Slowly, like he was sleepwalking, he stepped toward the tangled monster and walked right into its mouth—a huge black hole. The Terrible Tangle swallowed him up and licked its lips!

Dad was gone!

I sat up, panting. My pajamas were damp against my skin.

"You're okay. Just a nightmare. I'm here," Mom said, squeezing my hand. "You were thrashing and screaming in your sleep. Poor Nahla got a fright."

I snuggled into Mom's hug. When my panting stopped, I told her about the Terrible Tangle that gobbled Dad up.

"You're worried about Dad. So am I. I'm really sorry for all the noise down there. I was frustrated at Dad. I'm guessing you feel like it was wrong to tell me what you saw, but it was exactly the right thing to do." She kissed my forehead. "I want you to understand this isn't your fault."

I nodded and snuggled in tighter.

"I'd like to take you to talk to somebody who helps kids not have any more nightmares. We'll get through this together. I promise." That sounded good to me.

A few days later, I went to see a psychologist named Dr. Sam. He asked me to tell him about everything that was bothering me.

I shrugged. "I never see Dad anymore. He's always on his laptop. I miss him playing board games with me and eating dinner with us. He promised he'd help me figure out how to do flips on the trampoline."

Dr. Sam gave me some markers and a piece of paper and asked me to draw what scares me. I could have drawn Great Aunt Moyra's brussel-sprout-surprise casserole, but instead, I drew the junk in the trunk and the Terrible Tangle with all its windy legs and arms.

"It gobbles up people who stare at it." I pushed the picture away from me. "In my dream, it ate Dad in one bite." Would Dr. Sam laugh at my nightmare or brush it off?

He whistled. "Whoa. That must have been a very scary dream, Jaden." I nodded. Dr. Sam went on. "When kids see unsafe pictures or movies, it can be very confusing. It's normal to feel weird. That's probably why you had the scary dream. But talking with a safe adult can help." Hmmm. That seemed to make sense.

Later he asked if we could play catch together. He tossed the ball to me. "Sometimes, it can feel like we've done something wrong. Jaden, you didn't do anything bad."

I threw the ball back without saying anything. It felt good to let it go.

"It's okay to feel mad," he added, tossing the ball to me.

I caught it and stopped. It was weird that Dr. Sam said that. I'd felt bad because it seemed like this was all my fault. But he was right. Sometimes, I was so mad at Dad for hurting our family...

"Your dad has a problem that he can't figure out on his own. But he can get help for his problem. Your dad just has to ask for help. And all you have to do is ask for help." He nodded to my drawing. "Can I keep it?"

Fine by me. "I'll draw something not so scary next time."

He high-fived me.

When I got home, Dad was sitting on the front porch. I ran to him. "Dr. Sam was really cool. Next time..."

There was a suitcase beside Dad. Where was he going? It wasn't vacation time. I sat down beside him.

He was leaving. What could I say?

Dad pulled me to his side. "I'm sorry I haven't been good company lately."

"It's okay, Dad. You can stay," I said. "I don't want you to leave."

He shook his head. "I have a habit that's too hard to stop on my own. I need help, so I'm going to talk to a person like Dr. Sam. I'll be staying with Uncle Wes for a while, until I work it out. When I come back, I want to see that flip on the trampoline." He held up his hand for a fist-bump.

Dad was leaving us, but he'd be coming back. And he'd asked for help just like Dr. Sam said. That felt good—really good.

I glanced sideways at him. Would he really learn to stop spending so much time online?

I hoped so. We did a fist-bump together.

~~~~~~~~~~~~~~~~~

"Mom! Watch this—I finally got the flip figured out," I yelled from the trampoline up to the kitchen.

Mom came out on the landing, wiping her hands on a tea towel. The scent of apple pie followed her. "I'm coming. Just let me turn off the oven."

While I waited, I bounced a few times up and down, up and down, gaining enough height and speed to pull off a flip.

Up—tuck—flip—land. "Yesss!" A solid flip followed by an almost perfect landing. With a little more practice, I'd nail it.

Someone wolf-whistled and clapped, but it sure wasn't Mom. I stopped bouncing.

"Dad! You're back!"

"Hey buddy! That was the awesomest flip I've ever seen you do."

I rolled off the trampoline and ran to Dad. I hugged him with all my might.

He squeezed me and kissed the top of my head. "Oh man, I missed you and Mom so much."

Mom was smiling. That was nice to see.

"Are you staying home?"

"Sure am," Dad said. "I've had some ups and downs, but I've figured out some stuff—we can always learn new skills, just like you!" He patted the trampoline. "How about showing me another one of those flips?"

I scrambled back onto the mat. "You bet. And after that, we've got some apple pie waiting for us."

~~~~~~~~~~~~~~~~~

Ever since Dad got help and came back home, I see a lot more of him. We play board games and read stories before bed. He thinks my flips are getting better and better.

He is, too. Dad and Mom don't argue as much.

Best of all, the junk in the trunk—and the nightmare of the Terrible Tangle—are gone for good!

The End

Empowering books to prevent porn harm for kids learning to navigate the online world.

youngandaware.com

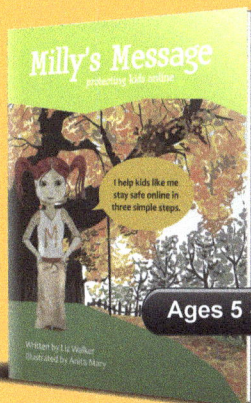

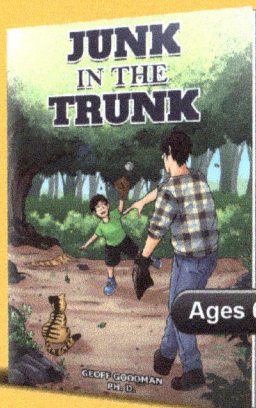

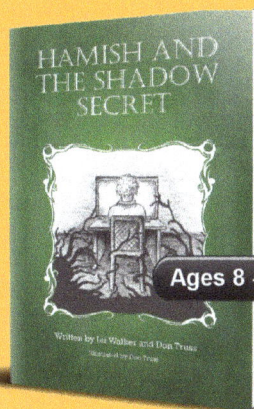

available at

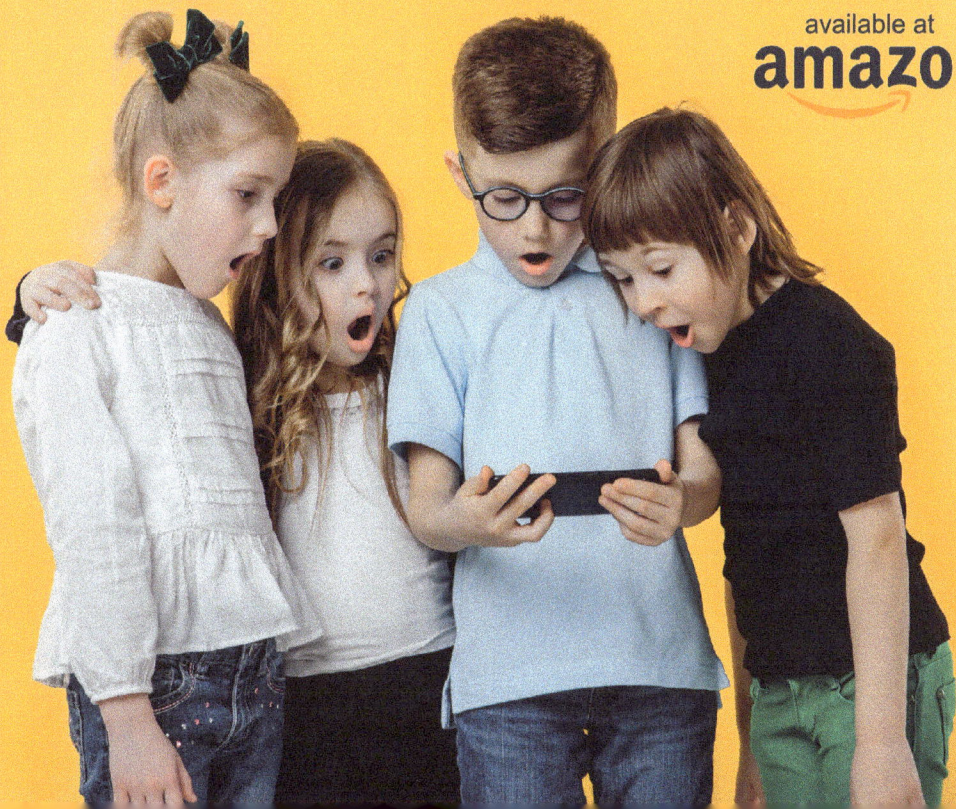

Parents, therapists, pediatricians, and other professionals working with children can find support notes and an educational conversation with Dr. Goodman at trunkbook.info.

. . . .

Young and Aware support the prevention of online porn harm through educational books, curricula and workshops.

When our young are aware of how porn harms through proactive and protective conversations, they are equipped to make safer choices.

Young and Aware educate to counter porn's messages and prepare our young for safe and healthy relationships.

Learn more at youngandaware.com

www.ingramcontent.com/pod-product-compliance
Lightning Source LLC
Chambersburg PA
CBHW041302040426
42334CB00028BA/3125